Author's Note

Thank you to all involved in helping me to create this poetry book. This process took me on an inner journey and allowed me to explore myself, past, present, and future. Many of you held my hand whilst I stared at my true self and remembered the depths of who I am and where I came from - so thank you for being the anchor I needed to keep me grounded throughout this journey.

Thank you to Neelam Saredia-Brayley, Nicola Everett, Rosie Parry-Thompson, Sophia Bloomfield, Chloe Carrington, Terina Gordon, Priscila Hernandez, Rhiannon Pitt, Katie Magrino, Bethanie Shepherd, and all who had helped me during my final year of university with their endless edits, proofreads, encouragement, and support throughout this process.

Thank you to my daughter for reminding me why I work hard and push my self everyday. Finally, to my love Sebastian Hernandez for encouraging me everyday to continue to do what I enjoy - writing.

Thank you.

Reflection

To the girl you were,
the daughter you are,
the mother you will be.
To a past you cannot change.
To the woman you became.

CONTENTS

Introduction.. 13

Prey 17

Parasite 51

Natural Selection 73

Survival 89

Alpha 105

Introduction

Biological Father:

> Life was the only gift you gave me;
> a beautiful white canvas.
> I spent years painting it and
> honing my craft.
> Don't come back.
> Your return would only spoil the picture.

Ex. X's. X:
The previous.
The last.
The past.
Nameless X
The X i drew to cross you out.
The X i drew to signal my mistakes
and mark the start of a new beginning.

Men:

> Your dick doesn't add inches to your personality,
> *sometimes.*
> Although, it can arouse a smile,
> *sometimes.*

Male Privilege:

> You camouflage in currency,
> Hide under biology.
> You think you're invisible,

but we see you.
in your mortal shroud –
boring, outdated, taking up
too   much   space.
There isn't enough room for you in this century,
and death
takes us all.

***

Am I the prey?
Well, in the circle of my life I've
had a taste of what it is like to be loved by a man.
so, I let them take me
and i rarely fight back.
But, they will never be the Alpha of this pride.

Maneater?
A fatal attraction to the taste of that love.
Fuelled with adrenalin;
with beautiful pain,
with feeling.
In the circle of my life
I chase the same man
as a dog chases his tail.
I take the bait and bite,
and the victory always hurts
as much as the last.

'A king is but a man; a queen is but a woman; a woman is but an animal; and an animal not of the highest order'.

~Edmund Burke, Reflections on the Revolutions in France, 1790

PREY

National Survey of Sexual Attitudes and Lifestyles poll

'The responses showed that nearly 40% of young women and 26% of young men did not feel that their first sexual experience had happened "at the right time".

Most had had sex by the time they were 18 - half had done it by the time they were turning 17. Nearly a third had sex before turning 16.'

~ Michelle Roberts, Health editor, BBC News:

Dear Diary

I have written a book. But, this book breathed herself to life. Diary, I called her. She lies beneath my pillow and I can feel her pulse rise and deflate with the weight of her breath. Sometimes, I cradle her in my chest and allow her to whisper her story softly in my ear. I let her sketch out the images, and I colour in the details. Sometimes, she tends to go too fast - draws the sketch, adds the detail, blends the shadow and splashes in the colour so I can't keep up. Those times I have to return her hard back beneath my pillow, and she panics. The harder I push her down the more she struggles for air. Eventually, she calms down and her slow release of breath returns. Like the placenta she gives me the nutrients I need to grow, and in return I remove the waste from entering her future. We need each other to survive.

I am lying in bed with a purple biro pressed against the page. I relay my first ever day trip to the local high-street alone. At eleven years old I approached the checkout at Woolworths and let the feeling of independence vibrate across my skin. I placed the ten-pound note in the lady's hand and waited for my change.
The scent when boarding the bus home was of musky cigarette from the man who stepped on after me. He trudged through the bus wearing a big puffy coat and trailed the smell of dead ash behind him. He sat beside an African lady who looked at me and screwed her face so that all her features were pinched and placed a long-nailed finger beneath her nostrils. She looked at me and I smiled to show my understanding. She returned my smile with another scowl before looking out of the bus window.

I am now twelve years old explaining how nervous I am to start secondary school. Doodles in the margin describing my new uniform; a black blazer and stripy tie. I practised how to knot a tie for days after deciding it must be done short and loose like the girls I saw when I visited the school.

A few days later I have my first squeeze of juicy gossip. A dark skinned boy with bright white gleaming teeth approached me at the front of the classroom. His friends stretched their necks in all directions watching for his next slick move. He asked for my number in front of the whole class and I became hooked bait to my own need of attention. When I got home, me and my diary devised a plan to roll my skirt up higher and unbutton my shirt collar. I asked to borrow one of mum's handbags for school the next day. She said no.

I write a few months later, announcing that he is now my boyfriend, but frantically scribbling his words, "if you don't perform for me soon then it's over, because Keira", another more popular girl at school; his ex-girlfriend, "performed for me all the time when we were together, so now we're together you have to too".

Again I visit my diary and I smudge the black pen so the writing is illegible. But I remember a crowd of his friends surrounded us barking orders. Someone pushed my back towards him as he leant against the corridor wall and waited. It was time for me to get my act together and perform.

"Kiss! Kiss! Kiss! Kiss!" they chanted.

"She won't do it," he whispered with a smirk, shaking his head and puffing out his chest, still leant with his back against the wall.

"I knew she was frigid!" yelled another member of the crowd.

"Dump her, she's boring!" heckled another.

I stepped toward him and drew a large dark bubble around us. The voices became blurred echoes, and the faces shaded black beyond the screened dome. Inside, he grabbed my face with one hand and slid the other up my skirt as if it were only us inside the cage. As if the crowd no longer towered around us. A second hand pierced through the barrier I created and slid its hand up my skirt. The bubble burst instantly and the crowd, like splatters of black tar, stained the floors of the corridor.

I remember boys blowing me kisses when I walked past, and girls serving poisonous gifts of raised upper lips and rolling eyeballs as replacement for my dignity.

The page is dirty and stained with muddy ink. The clean white leaf defiled and replaced with filthy words and foreign people who didn't belong within the safety of its sheets.

I am 13 years old and falling in love again. Describing our kisses and signing our married names across the pages.

I miss two months of writing.

*

My little book; My diary took her first breath. The first time she began to whisper her stories in my ear. The moment I birthed a new chapter and the book was reborn. I wish the pages wouldn't move me when I tried to read them.

The empty pages are replaced by images of me and a boy fooling around beneath the staircase at school. He passed a blackcurrant sweet from his mouth to mine and I could taste the warmth of his body. I inhaled the black earthy smell of his leather jacket blended with cigarette smoke whenever he walked past. There was nobody else like him there. His hair swung below his ears, and his trousers were always a little too big for him.

The pages are filled with the sound of his voice deeper and huskier than the other boys our age. His voice made me nervous, so I would laugh involuntarily whenever he spoke and told myself it was cute. Boys like cute. I can see his fingers stroking my knuckles and the shapes his lips made when he laughed.

When he invited me to his house for the first time the butterflies attacked the walls of my stomach. We stood in the centre of his room and I waited for his next move. The rising fear when he unbuttoned my school shirt, and lay me across his bedroom floor. Words didn't have the courage to show up, but talking was never a part of his fantasy.

It's the moment I stopped breathing. I decided to lie there immobile and not say a word. *We all have to have sex sometime; If I don't do it now then maybe I never will; I will look stupid if I stop now; he will tell his friends and everyone will laugh so I won't say a word. I'll stay still. Stop breathing.*

*

It's memories of me on the bus home, wishing I never went. The empty pages are stopped abruptly with dark blue marker pen drowning the white in a rough sea of scribbles. The trail of the pen, up and down, left and right without a beginning or an end.

In between the passing months, this living breathing notebook where the girl lives, is exhausted. She cuts it, abuses it, tears through its pages. The leather has lesions all over. I am sure I can see blood soaked through the binding. It screams and it cries, and I can feel its heavy breaths as it struggles for air underneath my mattress.

When I open the book, the girl looks so alone. She writes every evening about her day. She writes about how many guys she is talking to, and how she should look if she goes to meet them. Never back out at the last hurdle, she must go through with it all. *As long as they leave happy. As long as they leave happy.*

I can't read her book at all now. It's broken. The pages are all damaged and crinkled, but its heart still beats steadily. The cuts and slashes have healed their raw edges, and the blood has begun to dry. Every time I open the book, I can tell the spine can't take being read any more, but she still wants to speak to me. So I let her whisper her story softly in my ear. I let her sketch out the images and I colour in the details. If she goes too fast I have to push her hard back into my pillow. She gives me the nutrients I need to grow, and in return I remove the waste from her future.

We need each other to survive.

"The end," she whispers.

You Didn't Know

You didn't know how I felt,
when you held my hand.
I paused to absorb the warmth of your palms.
Each time you tensed your grip,
I held my breath to feel it.

You didn't know that
every time I laughed,
I saw my smile through your eyes.
Like a chameleon,
I changed my colours to match your favourites.

You didn't know,
when you held me from behind
I shrunk myself inches smaller.
Dainty enough for you to protect;
an ornament.
I wanted you to see how easy I am to break.

You didn't know the moment
you entered me.
        I cried.
You took more than I wanted to give,
and, I still gave you everything.

The next day,
when you spread the news of your fortune,
threw a lit match to anything expendable,
your friends collected the cremated pieces of me.
They scattered the ashes through the hallways.
They breathed them into my ears, my hair, my mouth

to keep me choking.

Didn't you know their words would burn too?
Like the blade I dragged across my flesh,
to gain control of the pain.
Words like spitting fire
singeing every hair
that used to stand on end when we touched.
When you stole your heart back,
you took mine too,
and I used my blood as commodity to retrieve it.

I didn't know
the places on my body where you once held me
would be the same places
I scraped red raw with a sponge
to stop myself from feeling you.

I didn't know the one thing you wanted
was irreplaceable.
You had your prize and your victory
sung like a chorus.
But I became the figure in an everlasting rhyme:

Slag. Slut. Dirty. Disgusting. Hoe. Whore.
Desperate.

Did you know word of mouth spreads like wildfire?
Flames blazed through the corridors.
Magma dripped from the lips of old friends.
I hated my body for the third degree burns that spelt the word shame.
"Kill yourself," they said.
"You're ugly," they said.

The words that fed me
crawled around the lining of my stomach.
Fingers jabbed at my tonsils to release them.
I regurgitated the words into my reflection,

"You're ugly," I said.

Boys shook your hand.
Girls saw your charm.
They tried to show you
where you went wrong with me.
They tried to show me
where I went wrong in thinking
I could be loved by you.
But, you knew that didn't you?

I became a canvas for hate.
You placed a blank slate
across my face
so people could deface it.
There was no need to see who was underneath.

Side stares, whispers, heckles,
pushed me, punched me, pulled at my hair.
Your covert aggression.
You used your friends as parrots
for your painful words.

Arms around my shoulders,
pulled down my trousers,
tripped me up,
pinched my bum,
hands up my skirt.

No means yes.
Yes means whore.
Stop means go.
And if you didn't know then,
well,
now you know.

<u>HOW DO YOU FEEL</u>

Written by

Ashanti T Bloomfield

FADE IN:

INT. TOWN COUNSELLING CENTRE - MORNING

Girl, 14, in school uniform with shirt hanging out
and hair in a messy bun. Girl is sitting on the
chair biting her nails and visibly fidgeting.
Screws up her eyebrows, shakes her head, closes her
eyes and bows her head down slightly.

> GIRL
> I just want it all to stop.

Councillor is sat up straight with legs crossed,
holding a pen and biting the end. Does not change
position throughout scene.

> COUNSELLOR
> And, how do you feel about that?

Girl Shrugs shoulders, does not change facial
expression.

> GIRL
> Mmm...

There is a long pause. Councillor raises an eyebrow
waiting.

> COUNSELLOR
> And, how do you feel about that?

> GIRL
> "I don't know."

> COUNSELLOR
> And, how do you feel about that?

> GIRL
> Empty.

Councillor looks at the clock, audibly breathes
out, loud enough for girl to look at her strangely.

She realises how loud her breath out is and attempts to blend the exhale into her next sentence.

                    COUNSELLOR
     Have you tried to visualise your emotions?

Girl raises an eyebrow and smiles mockingly.

                      GIRL
          Visualise?

Councillor begins to say sentence and then her words become slower and quieter, fading off mid-sentence.

                    COUNSELLOR
     Yes, sometimes it helps to visual-

                                    FADE TO:

INT. GIRLS BEDROOM - FlASHBACK.

ANGLE WIDE SHOT SHOWING ALL FOUR BEDROOM WALLS.

Every evening when the shadows beat the walls, Girl stares deep into the dark until it reveals colour. Until the silence begins to echo whispers, then words; laughter then sniggers. The silence smirks and eyeballs Girl whilst she walks through the black path it has paved for her. It spreads rumours.

                  UNKNOWN VOICE
                  (WHISPERING)
          No one likes you.

Wardrobe door swings open and hits the curtain next to it. A voice comes from it directed towards the curtain.

                  WARDROBE DOOR
     She doesn't wash her clothes you know.

CAMERA CLOSE UP TO THE WINDOW.

It is dark through the window. Every now and then Girl could hear a car drive past and the netted curtains are always kind enough to let the light enter through its web. They all smile at Girl and she lets her eyelids fall heavy as the light fades with the departure of the car. Then, the darkness welcomes Girl back in once more.

ANGLE WIDE SHOT SHOWING FULL BEDROOM

CURTAINS

I know, I heard she's got chlamydia.

Duvet attempts to defend her by ruffling at the top and bringing itself closer to her chest.

DUVET

No she doesn't!

A dark navy blue parka coat, now black in the depths of her bedroom. Coat is hanging from the door and lifts its sleeve pointing to the curtains.

COAT

Well, that's what I heard.

DISSOLVE TO:

INT. SCHOOL CORRIDOR - FLASHBACK.

ANGLE DISTANT BIRDS EYE VIEW OF CORRIDOR SHOWING STUDENTS BUSTLING THROUGH

Shannon, 14, Hair in a messy pony tail and wearing a scruffy uniform with a ladder up her tights. Shannon grazes Girl's coat sleeve when she shoves past her in the corridor.
Shannon turns around and sniggers at Girl whilst speaking. She then facetiously pokes fingers down her throat to mimic vomiting.

                         SHANNON
     Stay away from her Kelly, I've heard
     she's got chlamydia.

Kelly turns to Girl and elbows her gently with her
arm in a supportive manner. She gives her a half
smile.

                          KELLY
     Just ignore her.

                                            CUT TO:

INT. TOWN COUNSELLING CENTRE - AFTERNOON - PRESENT

                        COUNSELLOR
     If you can visualise your emotions. Maybe give
     them a colour, or a small shape, and imagine
     your self putting them in a box. This is
     supposed to help you get closure.

                          GIRL
     I see.

                        COUNSELLOR
     How do you feel about that?

Girl shrugs her shoulders and looks away.

                          GIRL
     Hmm.

                                          FADE OUT

Skin and Soul

Sometimes my skin
is the only one who listens.
The only one who can mimic my words exactly,
so I know she's understood.

My skin responds,
me too
and for a few minutes I can use her
as a vessel for my suffering.

Sometimes, my skin screams
OK, that's enough!
But, in the same breath asks for more.
As if she's thick enough to shield us both.
As if she's rough enough to fight back.
As if she's strong enough to carry it all.
In the end
she is always too weak to say stop and mean it.

We have a mutual understanding
my skin and I.
The downfall is,
I can't love her
the way she loves me.

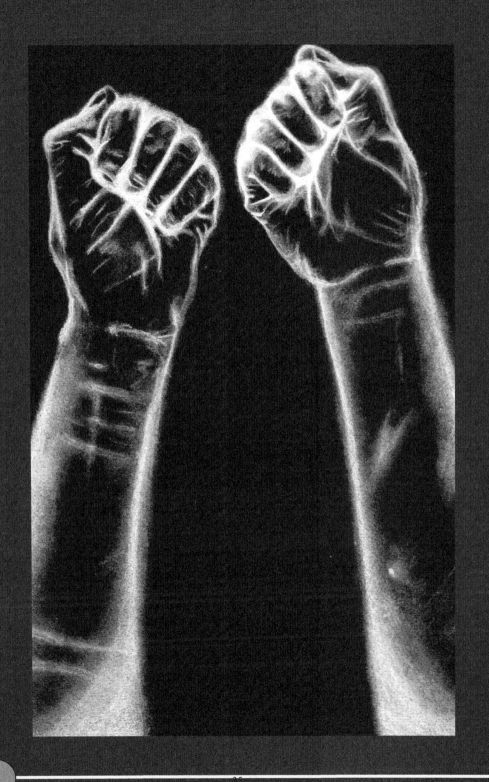

Attention Seeker

I imagine myself screaming from
the bottom of a deep well.
I hear the echoes of footsteps above.
Gossips say:
she put herself there.
She's just seeking attention.
But the truth is. I am.
I am in need of attention
Can somebody help me?
Where is everyone?

Wishes would fall on the crown of my head
and I'd try to throw them back up but
I could never throw them far enough.
If I could, maybe someone would see my worth.
Maybe someone would shout down and say,
"Climb up from the darkness,
let us take a look at you".
And I'd say
"I will, I just need some help! Could you throw me a rope?"
And they would.
Maybe I'd use it.
Maybe,
I'd
use
it

Below The Surface

My depression battles with me.
It pushes my head beneath the water
in a panic to survive.
I fight back but struggle to breathe.
The weight is too heavy to stay afloat.
I watch the air escape my lips
in frantic bubbles.
To speak would be to swallow
gulps of salt water and let it
anchor my body deep where the rocks lie.
To stay silent is to suffocate slowly.
I
sink
lower
and
lower
into the bed of the sea.
A sea filled with carcasses, just like mine.
I am desperate to pull my lifeless body
from this icy cold abyss. but,
I am stuck like muck at the bottom.
On land,
depression roams in my place,
A hollow shell since my soul lost its home.

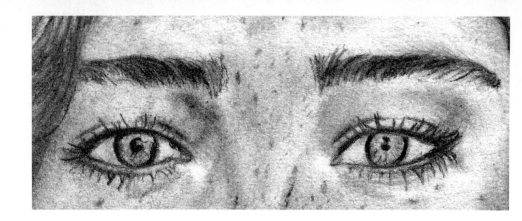

Yours

You realised my face didn't belong to you
so you branded it.

Knuckled MINE across my cheek,
and smiled.

Lifted my chin, stroked my jaw with your thumb,
and smiled.

I didn't need to speak the words.
You could read them in my eyes.

"Yours" they said,

and I smiled.

His

Like a predator,
you drain the fight from my veins.

Clamp my mouth shut
with the vice of your words.

Tighten it and watch me wince.
You part your lips. Lift your tongue.

Pause.

Fire your weapon.

Words:
>   you spit them at me.
>   you stamp them on me.
>   you cut them through me.
>   you take them from me.

Like a predator,
you watch and wait for movement.

But the only words left on my pale lips are
I'm sorry.

Toxic

Toxic is the colour yellow.
A soft pastel yellow.
The colour that blanketed my body
as the wind blew up my dress,
and I struggled to pin it down.
It was the yellow that you liked
when you told me I looked beautiful.

Toxic is the colour blue.
A dark midnight blue that hid us within four walls.
When you cuddled me
and cushioned my cheek into your biceps
I'd face the grainy blue paint and
gently graze my thumb against it.
Blue felt cool against my skin.
Blue felt safe.

Toxic is the colour grey.
A coarse, musky grey tearing holes through my leggings
when we sat on the ground smoking cigarettes.
The ground buried our secrets beneath us and
we planted roots within us.

Soon the roots began to blossom,
vibrant flowered pink petals
with soft dewy buds in the middle.
People-like-insects were attracted to the pretty flowers.
Insect-like-people plucked at the buds.
But we fought them off.
I stayed to watch them grow into something beautiful.

I watered them daily.
But the image of you was distorted through the liquid.
Rippled in awkward directions my eyes struggled to follow.
It began to turn dark blue.
Spilling and soaking into the musky tarmac
turning it a sharp, wicked grey.

The sun glistened on the ground's rough surface,
shooting a bright light toward my eyes.
It should have hurt and deflected my gaze.
But it didn't; I stared harder.

Toxic is the colour blue.
A deep haunting blue
cast by your shadow which stood over me.
Toxic is the colour blue
I can vaguely see it on the wall behind you
Your face is fierce and wet.
Your grip is a tight clasp of my shoulder.
Your grip is a tight clasp around my neck.
My fists graze against the grainy blue paint.
My back is cool against the wall.

Toxic is the colour yellow
I remember it through sorry words.
I remember it in the weeds that grow amongst the flowers.
I remember it when you cushion me in your biceps
and breathe in my hair.

I have no more secrets to share.
They're yours now.
You whisper your regrets through croaky cries,
and tell me you don't deserve me,
and you're right.

Toxic is so beautiful until you get a taste.
And even while I lick my lip and taste the blood
Toxic still seems so beautiful.

Mind

I only hear voices. I only feel voices. My Senses numbed by the pain of voices. I carve the voices. Skin deep voices. No! Soak them deeper. I wear the voices. I share the voices. I obey the sound of oppressive voices. They're shouting voices. They're doubting voices. Their voices corrupt our minds with poison. They're spiteful voices. Commanding voices. I answer only, to the voices. I lie with the voices. I talk to the voices. I collect the voices. Can you hear the noises? No one can. Just my own secret voices. Intrusive voices. Burying voices. Suffocating, deafening, damaging voices.

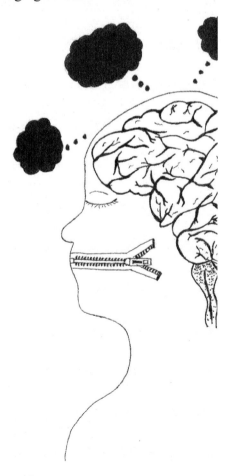

A Cycle

Sorry if my trauma leaves a bad taste in your mouth.
It tastes bad in mine too so I spit it out.
I reject it from my lips
so it doesn't sit
too long.
It's more than I can chew
so, I let some slip
down my throat and I swallow. Gulp.
It swims around my stomach,
a churning washing machine,
I can't switch it off whilst it ruminates.
I watch it spin and spin and spin,
then stop.
I know you saw it too -
the spinning.
We all watched it together.
You asked me how I'm doing
so I let the words bounce
off the buds of my tongue.
"I'm OK" I say.
Then, I take a seat to watch the next cycle.

<u>The Spiral</u>
Priscila
Hernandez
2019

A Maneater's Prey

I prowl the city after nine. The moon plasters my sleek shadow across corners of tall buildings. My skin is static from the silk that grazes across my curves. Black to minimise risk of being seen. A leg peeks through the slit of my skirt to cover more land in confidence. But I was unaware; carnivores mark this territory and they sense my presence before I can hide. I sit on some steps, pull out my phone and pretend to dial a number, but they can see me. The threat approaches as its tires squeal against the curb, crushing rocks beneath them. Windows slide down and the bass of the music pounds the ground beneath me. High pitched wolf-whistles, car doors slam shut, footsteps stomp upon my tracks to hunt me down. I see shadows approaching. Then I see him. He stands at the front of his pack smiling at me. They all wait and stare. Eyes navigate my curves and attack the fabric across my breasts. The wind betrays my hidden leg and supplies this carnivore with an invitation. Without a word he sits beside me. He strokes my thigh and the hair on my skin lifts in arms to protect me, but like a soft blanket for his tips, they spread. He weaves his hand through my coat and waits for me to flinch. I tried to stay still, to become road kill. But, my body shakes in cold sweats as he slips his hand down by shirt, cups my breast in his hand and squeezes. Like a hyena he grins, still weighing the fullness of my breast in his hand. He swipes my nipple and smiles as they perk. He mutters words and his pack laughs with him. He glides his hand out, knocks me on the chin with his knuckles, turns around and struts back to his car. He doesn't look back. He drives away leaving the sound of the engine humming in my ears on the slow, painful walk home.

***

I prowl the city after nine. Wounds begin to heal after time. I recover the land I marked in confidence and make it mine once again. It is late. Myself and a friend are on our way back home from a long night of clubbing. I wonder why a kebab only tastes good when I'm drunk or hungover, and It makes me laugh. I turn to my friend and she smiles at me. I look at her lips, wet after licking them, her teeth aren't as white during the day. I search her smile for the warmth and comfort she is offering, but all I find in the creases of her cheeks are the memories of him. Her quizzical glare watches my breath beat the cold air in rapid punches. I cup my chest and begin to hear the humming of cars as they drive by.

'The why a refined, physically fragile woman will mate with a brute, a mere male animal with primitive passions - and love him [..] they have all overlooked the eternal wildness, the untamed primitive savage temperament that lurks in the mildest, best woman. Deep in through the ages of convention this primeval trait burns, an untameable quantity that may be concealed but is never eradicated by culture'

~ George Egerton, A Cross Line, 1893

PARASITE

INSTRUCTION

MANUAL

- Requires 2 people
- Please ensure all pieces

  are present before

  unpackaging model

CONTENTS

Model Diagram.............45
Instructions...................46 - 47
Testimonial...................48 - 49

Model Diagram

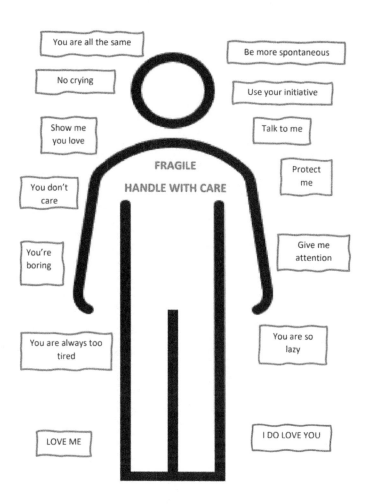

You are all the same

No crying

Show me you love

You don't care

You're boring

You are always too tired

LOVE ME

Be more spontaneous

Use your initiative

Talk to me

Protect me

Give me attention

You are so lazy

I DO LOVE YOU

FRAGILE

HANDLE WITH CARE

Instructions

General Safety Rules:

This Model is intended to be as a companion through life.

Please handle with care to reduce the risk of toxicity.

Once partnership is initiated, Model can experience mood swings which may or may not subside.

Please Note: Model is pre-made with "free will" and can choose to:

1. Leave.

2. Disagree.

3. Display aggressive and/or violent behaviour.

4. Be inclined to display laziness.

5. Be inclined to display stubbornness.

6. Be inclined to display complacency.

- **Complacency** is most common after the first year of companionship, moving into home together **and/or** after first child.

For more details on Models affected with free will issues, please consult magazines such as *Cosmopolitan, Women's Weekly, Elle, or Take a Break*. This will help with occurring problems with Model, or offer any information regarding general the behaviour of Model.

In any case please refer to this manual to determine if issues occurred in:

1. The manufacturing process of Model.

2. Any presuppositions of Model's personality.

3. Forgetfulness of Model's free will installation, which may cause rejection of manipulation.

4. Rose-tinted glasses worn at time of construction.

In addition, Model is installed with **affection, helpfulness, support, and care.**

If Model is well suited to you, these traits will be well exposed.

If not, these traits will appear in flickers.

If flickering is shown please **DO NOT** blink too often; there is high possibility of missing said traits.

<u>NOTE:</u> **Once 'love' is given to Model, no refund nor exchanges can be provided. The heart cannot erase the strong connection of 'love' and must be handled with care. Removal of Model is possible, but 'love' is not easily forgotten.**

Model may display dependent tendencies which include:

1. Belief you are surrogate mother.

Please Note: Model is NOT at fault.

Stereotypical expectation of female is to:

1. Wash clothes and dishes.

2. Cook.

3. Clean.

4. Iron.

5. Display maternal and angelic tendencies.

6. Nurse and diagnose.

7. Remember everything (no specificity as to what).

- For the purpose of this manual we have had to select a non-exhaustive list. To view the extended version of this list, please visit a local library and look up women's history and patriarchal ideals of female sex.

If female is to conform to female stereotype and perform these acts regularly, Model is *incapable* of understanding this is not female duty. Model is not at fault.

Testimonial: Faulty model

How do you miss an absent-
Something you never-
I don't know.

When the kids at school asked me
Where's your dad?
I would hold my breath, shrug my shoulders. Wait
'I don't have one'.

They tilt heads in confusion,
hands slapped to mouths.
Eyebrows raised.

How do you find the *right* man
with no model to guide you?
Daddy issues.
Sew the perfect man,
from the fabric of my father's mistakes.
I buried the word father in the ground at a young age.
Lost hope suffocates within its coffin.
Abandonment.

Curiosity clawed its nails at the soil
to find what lay more than six foot deep
In the dark pit of my mind.
I excavated his carcass at the age of nineteen,
I tried to restore the rotten flesh to the bones.
Dressed his skeleton in patchwork of
why wasn't I enough?
Did you think about me?

I imagine the bicycle I had as a child,
riding through the gaps in the stitching.
My mother supporting the handle-bars.

Exhumation and attempt at restoration complete,
the bones collapsed to the ground.
I attempted to understand
the cause for his lack of stability.
But I realised
he wasn't built correctly.

Mother didn't tell me that
all men were cut from a *different* cloth.
When the kids at school asked me
        Where is your dad?
I should have told them,
his spine was missing.
I should have buried him much earlier.

Silence

The lights are off.
Nobody is home.
Your eyes are windows
But they're too dark to see inside.
I peak through a gap in the curtain.
I can see your silhouette.
You bounce your head to the beat of your own tempo.
I press my ears against your walls.
I can't get close enough to hear it but
I can feel it beating.
It rattles the window frames.
I watch my breath escape my lips
and evaporate with the cold air.
The lights are off.
You are home.
But you won't come to the door.

Expectations

I spent years trying to build a home for us.
But, It kept falling apart.
The bricks were solid.
But, the foundation weak.

I kept building and
eventually I built it too big.
I stood alone in large rooms echoing large fantasies.

People always say
dreams do come true
if you work hard enough.
So I spent some time with my eyes closed,
dreaming.

If I tightened my lids hard enough
If I worked hard enough
If I build and build,
you will make my dreams come true.
You will help me keep this home standing.

But you never did come to visit.
When all went dark,
I had to find the fuse to bring back the spark.
Alone I changed the light bulbs;
cleaned the house;
bought the furnishings.

After another lonely day in the dead room.
You finally knocked on my door and
asked me how my day was and

If I needed a hand.
I said, no thank you.
You can't help me when only I can see the dream.

Indulgence

I trap your body between my legs because
I know it's where you want to be.
Slip my tongue through your mouth
in search of words to quench my thirst for affection.
But you're empty.   So I am too.

I spread my body on the table like a banquet
ready for you to dive in.
I lie like a steak of the best cut,
rare and soft.   Underdone.
Overcome with greed,
you forgot to save any for me.

I am starving.
I need you to feed me.
Cram the letters,
b-e-a-u-t-y, l-o-v-e, s-t-r-e-n-g-t-h,
between my lips and
wait for me to swallow.
Self-deprecation strangles my appetite.
But I know I am hungry
because the letters look so beautiful
on everyone else.

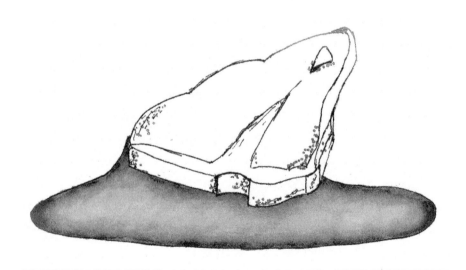

Wallpaper

I am not the wallpaper.
Glue does not attach me to this home.
Nor does the love which
floats in the air,
but never sets. This
wallpaper is not yellow, So,
stop trapping me within its curves.
When you leave,
take me with you.
I will show you the air I breathe is real.
I am not patterned moquette. Designed
to conceal your footprints. Designed
to conceal my words. Designed
to conceal the marks caused by overuse and neglect.
I do have many colours, you may not have noticed
with your eyes glued to a screen.
I'll shock you with colours
you haven't discovered yet.
I am not here to sit in the background.
I am not the wallpaper.

Unspoken

Whatever you're not telling me
I can feel it.
Twisting muscles in my stomach,
tightening my lips
so the words can't escape my mind.
Words that run marathons around my brain
with no finish line;
I can feel it sitting on my chest.
cutting my breath
short.
Silence is deadly.
Speak to me.

"Life for both sexes - and I look at them, shouldering their way along the pavement - is arduous, difficult, a perpetual struggle. It calls for gigantic courage and strength. More than anything perhaps, creatures of illusion that we are, it calls for confidence in oneself".

~ Virginia Woolf, A Room of Ones Own, 1929.

NATURAL SELECTION

"The floor seemed wonderfully solid. It was comforting to know I had fallen and could fall no farther."

~ Sylvia Plath, The Bell Jar, 1963

A Scary Story

No one wants to hear the gory details.
Like when you switch on the news and
see who else has died today, and
quickly change the channel.
What is the next tragic thing that'll pollute our existence in horror
stories?
We only like horror stories when the tragedy isn't real.
When it moves across our TV's,
when we can hide our faces when it gets too gory.
No one wants to know where the story comes from.
The reality.
But I have to speak it from my mind.
So, cover your eyes if it is too real for you.

A miscarriage for me wasn't like the films:
a sharp pain to the stomach,
doubled over screaming for help;
a rushed trip to the hospital for the doctor to say
unfortunately my dear, you have lost the baby.

No.

A miscarriage for me was waking up peacefully,
but, a warm, moist texture between my legs.
It was staring at blood on my hands.
Instead of being told why,
already knowing the why.

Not understanding why.

It was turning my bathroom into a delivery room;
the toilet bowl, my midwife.
It was a cold shaking body in a hospital chair,
explaining the same story,
for the third time,
to the third poker-faced doctor.

It was remembering my baby and then
forcing myself to forget.
It was sore plump breasts left with no purpose.
The milk longing to satiate a hunger which no longer existed.
It was wishing I could unzip
my skin from my bones because
I couldn't scrape the stains from my hands.
It's bleeding day in day out and knowing what it is.
It's loving someone I never met.
It's hating them for leaving me without an explanation.
It's hating myself *just because.*

I can't hide from my body
the same way you hide from a horror film.
This nightmare is real.

A Bad Egg

The aftermath is waking up from a bad dream
at regular intervals throughout the day.

Staring at the frying pan on the hob.
Burning the eggs.

Consoling pregnant friends,
who are worried about their pregnancies
ending too soon.
Like yours did.
Congratulating them when it doesn't.
Playing spot the difference to see what you were missing.
Hoping that *next time* you will be
the full healthy package.
If there is a next time.

Scape the burned egg remains from the frying pan.
Crack another egg.
Start again.

Nightmares only live in the things you can't control.
So, if there is a next time.
This could happen again.
Oh no, I'll be more careful next time.
But, the doctor said it wasn't my fault.

Turn the hob off.

She was just trying to make me feel better
Bless her.
I'll be more careful next time.

Place the egg on the plate.

Glitch

There is a glitch in the system.
My smile loads half-
way.
Stops.
Then resets.
There is a glitch in the system.
This anti-virus called guilt
attacks the endorphins.
They've been fighting tirelessly to prickle my skin.
Error. Error. Error,
leaves static in my veins and
my legs go weak whilst my eyes fill with water.
System failure - I crash and
my happy thoughts burn as the guilt consoles my body.
Error message: G R I E F I S A P R O C E S S.

The Postnatal Bubble

When my daughter burst the bubble inside me
I thought she would slip right out.
If she could just wait a little while longer,
and give me a little bit more time.
But, there is no time.
The bubble of my childhood,
My selfish ways,
my me days.
Trips to the corner shop with just the breeze past my sides
burst and left me empty.

I was so happy with her in my belly,
excited to see that little face.
What happened?

Now let me tell you.
There were no moments of gazing into that newborns face,
that made my worries melt away.
No.
Every well wisher became the enemy,
I kept my eyes wide
whilst the world slept.
I stood guard to make sure she was safe.
Her breaths heavy and her belly puffed out.
Like a little bubble.

Like a sniper,
I stood at a distance.
I wouldn't let anything, or anyone pop her bubble.
 "Would you like to hold her?" My partner asked.
No.

But, I will watch over her.
I'll be her guardian angel so no one can hurt her.
But love her?
Not yet.
I haven't had a chance to grieve.

If she cried,
I would be by her side,
I will listen to the screams and tell myself I have to.
because I am her mother.

I would put a breast to her lips,
rock her to sleep,
sing her silly songs
because I am her mother.

Bathe her soft naked skin,
dress her and wrap her up for warmth.
Sleep little girl.
I will stay and watch over you.
The demons will have to go through me first.

Until then,
I'll just protect you.
I'll listen to your screams and cries,
I'll lock myself inside rooms and hide,
I'll curl into a ball at your side.
I'll keep fighting those demons at night.
My best will never be perfect
But, I will always try.
Because I am your mother.

Her	Him
Bends down,	Bends down,
collects the dirty washing,	Collects socks from drawers.
Throws them into wash basket	Slips them onto bare feet.
Sits in car,	Sits in the car,
Drives to work,	Drives to work.
Gets stuck in traffic,	Gets stuck in traffic.
Thinks about child at school.	Thinks about child at school.
Returns from work	Returns from work.
Tries to cook dinner	Sits at dinner table to eat.
Realises there is not enough food.	Realises it is third time that week
Takes deep breath,	eating pasta.
Rustles up the best meal she can.	Takes a deep breath.
Complains about the cleaning.	Thinks about lack of money.
No response	Complains about work.
Takes a deep breath.	Thinks about the lack of wage.

Her	Him

Her

Him

Takes a deep breath.
Complains there is no money.

Cleans house.
Plays with child,
Waits for child to finish bath.
Gives child a kiss good night.
Wonders if she is doing a good job
as a mum.

Argue with him
Go to bed.
Repeat the day from the top.

Complains there is nothing on
telly.
Thinks about how tired he is.

Relaxes.
Runs child's bath.
Plays with child.
Reads her bedtime story.
Wonders if he is doing a good
job as a dad.

Argue with her.
Go to bed.
Repeat the day from the top.

The Working Mother

Ring. Ring.
Ring. Ring
Music plays continuously.
02:05 seconds.
03:14 seconds.
Automated voice: If you would like to enquire about support with childcare, please visit, www.weareunhelpful.co.uk.
If you would like to speak to an advisor *(who is a fucking human)* for enquiries with support with childcare press 1. Press 2 if –
– BEEP.
Enter 1 into keypad.

Hello, my name is _____ how can I help you today.

Explain problem for several minutes.
14:03 seconds.

Have you thought about working more hours to reach the 16-hour free child-care help?

Re-explain and describe daily occurrences with 4-year-old child and school runs. Explain the added pressure of more hours which equals more childcare, which equals more childcare bills, which equal less pay, which equals zero logic.

I see. You could also be entitled to 30 hours free childcare support.

Explain 35-hour job that ends at 6pm daily, including summer holidays, bank holidays, half terms and weekends.
16:17 seconds.

Could you please hold the line while I speak to someone who may be able to help.

Music plays continuously
19:30 seconds
19:32 seconds
19:35 seconds

Hello Miss _____. Do you have a child with a disability?

Re-explain and describe daily lifestyle and child. End with a polite but slightly aggressive no.

I see. Unfortunately, we are unable to support you with childcare as you do not fill the criteria for help, and as your child turns 5 soon you will also be ineligible for the 30 free hours. I can suggest you...

Daydream – She can only suggest I wait until my child is 16 years old and able to take care of herself by which time my only experience would be with my child. I could study part-time and find a job that fits between school times. Yes, that is what I will do. Because I'm a mother and that is my main responsibility.

Is there anything else I can help you with Miss _____?

Say no because you understand your duty and hang up the phone. Answer child who is showing you a drawing they did at school and give them a cuddle.
Wait for husband/partner to return home from work and thank him for all he does – clean home and take care of child to measure up to his responsibilities.

Thank you Miss _____ Have a nice day.

Mags at the School Gates

When people ask,
But what about the father's
I say,

Haven't they had enough praise for their masculinity?

They've been praised for centuries,
But us women became martyrs for ours.
Starved themselves for ours.
Some are still starving.
I for one am famished.

Women had to fight.
But now we fight each other instead.
Who can be the best mother?
Doesn't the deciding vote go to our children?
I don't care what kind of mother
Margaret at the school gates thinks I am.

Oh wait, I do.

Because she looks down on me.
Because her child had a gold sticker at school.
Because mine had a red card for 'bad behaviour'
Because of course,
her husband,
The child's father, Is around and knows discipline.

But, what about the fathers?
Yes, Margaret
you fool.

Yes, Some fathers do their part and
yes, Some fathers do nothing at all and
yes, Many fathers are the sole carers of their children.

But, MARGARET! Listen.

I celebrate the women,
and I worship the mothers who carried them.
I fight with the women who are still fighting for recognition
Because our equality is still yet to be recognised.
It takes the equal match of man and woman to create life.
But, the population is born from a woman's womb,
Every man climbs out of a woman
and automatically has more power than his mother,
as if she deserves to birth her own oppression.

Yes, I am a feminist.
Yes, I am a mother.
Yes, I am a proud woman.

No, Mags I'm not saying you're not proud too.

I demand praise for our sacrifices.
I demand recognition of our equal rights,
the same rights that men were so very lucky to be born into.

'It was almost as unnecessary to cultivate doubt of oneself as to cultivate doubt of ones own best friend; one should try to be one's own best friend, and to give oneself, in this manner, distinguished company'.

~ Henry James,

A Portrait of a Lady,

1881

SURVIVAL

Moral Compass

We don't tell people that they are a waste of space, that they are too fat, too ugly, or too useless. So why do we say it to ourselves? Surely our own self-happiness is more important.

We beg the world to validate us, provide for us and comfort us, but when our minds and bodies ask the same of ourselves, we ignore it.

We walk through seas of bodies but rarely look at the body that carries us. We attempt to steal our neighbour's eyes to view ourselves, but the theft becomes a needless crime in vain. We depend on other people to explore our wants and needs and hope that they will protect us from harm. When we are in a room surrounded by people and we struggle on the inside, hoping somebody will notice, that is when we realise it. We realise that we are the only person who knows what's inside our minds. We are alone unless we share our deepest inner thoughts.

But, The moment we open our lips to share our thoughts, our dependencies grow larger, praying the listener, the friend, the brother, the sister, will provide us with the strength we are searching for. We expect them to rub our knee when we fall and tell us "It's all better now". They can try, but their words and comfort will never hold the power we hope it will. The power comes from within.

Guidance is a resource, not a crutch. We can use another's words as a compass to help us find ourselves, but we can't expect to ride on their backs along the journey. You were born innocent, you grow, you learn and become the person you are. Live life independently and provide for your soul in every way you can. You must nurture your soul. Anyone who asks to accompany you through your life's journey, allow them to be your compass and your friend rather than your crutch to keep going. They are a bonus, not an unhealthy habit of dependency.

Remember, there is only one of you in this world, and you have so much to offer. So learn to love yourself and remember people only come into your life as an addition, not a replacement for anything you feel is missing. You are perfect exactly the way you are.

Strength

"You're so strong."
Am I strong because you witnessed the victory
but didn't see the fight?
Life throws punches and knocks me to the ground.
Life mocks me as it nurses me in bed and says,

You'll get up, and when you're asked if you're okay you'll say
yes and smile.

Life tells me,

this isn't a journey for suckers,
Get up, do your job and live.
Crawl on your hands and knees
And cry through that tunnel until you make it.

Life helped me to the bathroom and
Told me it's okay not to wash,

There's always tomorrow.

Life beat me through the night and told me to sleep.
It said:

Wake up when you feel better
I'll wait for you.
There are some lessons I have to teach you,
So, sit the fuck up and learn.

Tell me, why am I strong?
I didn't have a choice but to take the punches.

Am I strong because I'm living like I was told to.
Am I strong because when you ask if I'm okay
I said yes and smiled, like were all shown to.
I thought only the prey are weak,
but life eats me alive anyway.
No matter how strong I look to you
That smile isn't mine.
Am I strong because eventually I told life

Fuck you!

I got up, did my job and lived.

I lived.

A Message

When you have been disarmed,
find a new weapon.
Reload and reclaim power.

When you feel as though your skin
is no longer comfortable enough to walk in,
Ask it what it wants.
Feed yourself love until it spills over.
Cater to yourself.
Dress yourself in anything you want,
Its all beautiful,
because its on *you.*

After a drought,
the rain will come.
Stand beneath it and shower yourself in the
memories of books that filled your mind with words,
but never enough to answer all of your questions.

Memories of the dewy glow that shone from your
skin
when you smiled into your reflection,
and realised you could see, what no one else could.

Memories of your child whose hand you held,
whose tears blended with your own, and
reminded you that strength doesn't have to be
physical.

Let the rain saturate your clothing, flood your mind, wash
away the doubt.
Repeat this process over and over
so it cannot be forgotten.
Because sometimes
it is easy to forget.

High Fashion

I spent many years searching for the perfect outfit.
Something to accentuate my beauty and
set myself apart from the rest.
I tried to accessorise my voice,
pronouncing the T's,
raising my tones to a higher pitch.
Tightened belts around my opinion.
Starved myself of words to allow my hollow carcass
to walk smoothly across eggshells.
Singed my hair with hot iron plates
to flatten out the kinks of my culture.
I spent many years searching for the perfect outfit.
But it took many more to realise,
perfection lies in the bruised, broken,
but beautiful skin I had all along.

Earth's Beauty

No people,
no voices
Just me and earth's beauty.
The sound of green leaves
brushing one another.
The sound of the wind sifting through trees.
The smell of the grass the mud and the rain.
The grey hue that tints the horizon.
The cold air that travels down my throat and expands my lungs.
The small smile on my lips.
The damp due on my cheeks.
The crisp wave of my hair.
No people,
no voices.
Just me and earth's beauty.

God is a Woman

The constant need to nurture the lips that part with a cry.
I hang my worries out to dry
after a long daily spin cycle in the pit of my stomach.
How many layers of the glass ceiling
does a mother have to shatter?
How many times must my wounds re-open from the
shards that slice, that scar, that insinuate,

you can't do it all

Wasted words.
The days are new, the life is ancient.
Woman.
Recycled, regenerated, reanimated,
born from Mother Earth's flesh.
Devoured by those who populate it,
I can seep like sap into the soil,
or I can help form a shield around earth's sisters
and reclaim the power we've always had.

Be Proud

Stop saying crying is weak!
Your tears are the result of a battle you are facing.
Without tears, life would look easy.
Life isn't easy.
I am proud of you.
Be proud of yourself for putting up a fight.
You are doing great.

Subconscious
Sophia Bloomfield
2016

Strengthen the female mind by enlarging it, and there will be an end to blind obedience; but, as blind obedience is ever sought for by power, tyrants and sensualists are in the right when they endeavour to keep women in the dark, because the former only want slaves, and the latter a play-thing.

Mary Wollstonecraft
A Vindication of the Rights of Woman
1792

ALPHA

Wake Up Questionnaire

Pay close attention to the notes to guide

you through

Many thanks,

Author.

WAKE UP

Please see Key Notes for all questions marked with (*) for help.

1. I am a   Mother ☐   Father ☐

2. I am   Woman ☐*   Man ☐   Other ☐

(i) Woman: Born or identify as the female gender.

3. I am   Employed ☐*   Unemployed   ☐

(i) Employed: Paid employment, self-employed or voluntary work.
(ii) **Unemployed:** Not employed in any kind of work.

4. I am a student   Yes ☐*   No   ☐

(i) Student: Studying any subject at any level; vocational or academic.

5. Single   ☐
    In a relationship   ☐
    Married   ☐

6. I am happy in my relationship status   Yes ☐   No ☐

(i) Happy: feel complete contentment, comfort and pleasure.
No desire **AT ALL** to change relationship status with person in question.

7. I am   16+ ☐   18+ ☐   25+ ☐

8. I like to wear.

Dresses ☐   Skirts ☐   Trousers ☐   Make-up ☐

Heals   ☐   Hats ☐   Bags ☐   Tracksuits ☐

Trainers ☐   Sandals ☐   Jewellery ☐   Tattoos ☐

(i) Clothing: Do any of these items determine whether you are a good or bad person?

9. I am sexually active   ☐*

(i) Sexually active: Any form of sexual activity, not limited to vaginal intercourse.

10. I have been a victim of sexual harassment ☐*

(i) Sexual harassment: unwanted sexual attention or advances, physical or verbal in a social or workplace setting.

11. I have been a victim of sexual assault ☐*

(i) Sexual assault: Any type of sexual activity or contact, including rape, that happens without your consent. Sexual assault can include non-contact activities, such as someone 'flashing' you (exposing themselves to you) or forcing you to look at sexual images - https://www.womenshealth.gov/relationships-and-safety/sexual-assault-and-rape/sexual-assault

12. I have the right to vote ☐*

(i) Vote: Have a say in political elections. If you tick the box, do you feel a sense of pride? Think, does everybody have this right? Should everybody have this right? Does this right make a difference to you? Do you care?

13. I have been hindered due to my sex or gender ☐*

(i) Hindered: ANY time in your sex or gender made life difficult in any way. ANY time your sex or gender made you feel inferior in some way.

14. I have been the oppressor ☐*

15. I have been oppressed due to my sex or gender ☐*

(i) Oppressed: been treated harshly, cruelly, unfairly, or stopped from doing something as a result of your sex or gender.

16. I am strong ☐*

(i) Strong: SUBJECTIVE – strength from within: physically, mentally, emotionally, or spiritually. Able to withstand any unwanted negativity.
Please note, when answering this question remember, we are all human.

17. I do household duties because I enjoy it Yes ☐ Other ☐*

(i) Household duties: Any responsibilities within the household. Duties done because they *had* to be, not for pleasure. Also, expected to do this as a result of your sex/gender.

18. I feel affected by the town I live in   Yes ☐*   No ☐

(i) Affected: Social and cultural expectations placed upon your sex/gender as a result of the place you live.

19. I feel supported by the government   Yes ☐*   No ☐

(i) Supported: Age, sex or gender, mother, father, guardian, employed, unemployed, student, single, married, cohabiting, disabled, low income, high income, home owner, private renter, homeless, ill mental health, ill physical health, healthy, taxpayer – **Applies to all.**

Please note, If you have ticked no, assuming you are not doing anything to change this - can you answer why you aren't doing anything to change this? Refer back to question 14 on your right to vote for a moment of reflection.

20. I have suffered mental ill health   Yes ☐*   No ☐

(i) mental ill health: Depression, anxiety disorders, schizophrenia, eating disorders, addictive behaviours alongside many more. Any illness that has impacted mental health negatively and impairs daily life.

21. I have a right to choose what happens to my body   Yes ☐*   No ☐

(i) Right to choose: All decisions relating to your body are made by you.

(ii) Has this right been debated by others in any way shape or form - regardless of this being your own body? *Have a think.*

22. My right to choose does not matter   Yes ☐*   No ☐

(i) Doesn't matter: SUBJECTIVE – you have the right to choose and control your own body. You cannot control the actions of other people (Reference to Alabama abortion ban) Also to consider this question please see notes for questions:
(12),(13),(14),(15),(16),(17),(20),(21).

Dog Eat Dog World

Women empower women.
Is this after,
Girls disempower girls?
Bitches try hard to be
man's best friend.
They mark their territory
Or consequently feel their teeth
pierce black holes through the harness
that once kept you safe.
Claw at your cloak of confidence.

Bitches are much like the studs.
Carnivores.
Bark hate and blame it on the season
Reminisce of *stupid times.*
Let's call the bullying puberty
That was years ago, we were so young
Just young pups.
they forget the scars their teeth left behind.

Now they fill *inspirational* quotes across social media.

 NEW POST:

"Newborn activists of suicide prevention"

Prevention?
I remember when you called it *seeking attention.*
That girl at school got your attention,
I remember you helped her hold the knife to her wrists

and *prevented* her from using it too softly.
Now you use social media
to save the next generation from suffering,
but you tell me to
save past for therapy
and stop dwelling

NEW POST:

"Mental Health Awareness"

But, students never pretend to be *unaware*.
They never fail to point at the girl
whose eating alone in the lunch hall.
They never fail to create distance because her silence
is *too weird* for their comfort.

NEW POST:

"Fight against body shaming."

But her flat chest was comedy gold in the classroom.
Teach girls to love themselves
After pressing dirty paws on all there was to love.

NEW POST:

"Black lives matter!"

Did it matter when *this* black life
was marginalised
by *other* black lives

for not sounding enough like
a black life?

Let us dig holes in the dirt and
bury the bones of the past.
Let us lick the wounds and move forward.

I'm sending a reminder
to all the bitches whose words and bullying
graffitied bodies with trauma and scars.
and now use social media to convince us of their growth
all I can say is,
congratulations on teaching the next generation
to be less like you

Bitches.

#publish charity for an award

Feminist:
Sex is not a boundary

S	G	S	G	G	V	W	E	A	L	T	H	Y	D
Y	P	N	E	N	A	I	A	I	T	Y	O	S	M
O	T	P	I	H	I	A	O	R	I	Y	L	A	A
T	P	A	Y	G	T	N	E	L	I	S	I	H	R
S	P	I	O	C	N	O	A	L	E	A	Y	E	R
T	P	A	C	L	T	I	L	E	A	N	H	E	I
A	U	O	R	E	A	D	S	C	L	E	C	O	A
Y	E	I	W	E	S	P	O	R	T	C	T	E	G
L	T	G	S	E	N	C	T	D	L	I	A	N	E
D	C	R	O	T	R	T	E	M	O	T	I	O	N
P	A	M	E	A	R	N	H	W	L	D	U	T	Y
R	S	N	E	V	L	E	Y	O	A	E	P	A	R
I	A	N	C	E	O	S	S	S	O	E	Y	N	H
I	A	R	E	E	W	P	L	S	E	D	A	R	Y

SPORT	MARRIAGE	NAILS
DANCE	EMOTION	WEALTHY
PARENTHOOD	VIOLENCE	HAIR
TOYS	PAY	GOALS
DUTY	CLEANING	POWER
CLOTHES	STRESS	RAPE
SINGING	POVERTY	

A losing battle

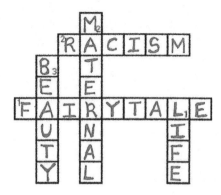

Across

1. Gender stereotype. Man and wife lived happily ever after. Human body as consumption to sustain the patriarchal appetite
2. Each breed suffers it. No breed unanimously stops it. Every breed bares the same bones. Battle of who is better. Demonstrations of who's scars are cut deepest. The creators won but their carcasses rot beneath the ground. Usurpers restore the legacy. But the war continues. Who is the winner?

Down

1. A journey with no guide. Hunters waiting around each bend. No way to curve the carnivores. Play dead wait for it to pass. You find happiness in the end
2. Mother as extension of child's mind and body. Mother does not feel unless child allows it. Mother does not make the mistake of being woman. Mother does not make the mistake of being human. Mother does not make mistakes
3. White. Light. Clean. Winter coat sparkles but lacks camouflage amongst the open plane. Most sought for. The image to replicate to gain the privilege of being acknowledged. Gene's cannot replicate stereotypes and social construct.

Across

1. fairytale
2. racism

Down

1. life
2. maternal
3. beauty

WOMEN'S ARCADE: THE PREQUEL

Word:
Definition – A single, distinct meaningful element of speech or writing.
   "Meaningful?"

Meaningful:
Definition – Having Meaning. Serious, important, or worthwhile.
   "Worthwhile?"

The glass ceiling will be "meaningful" in fragments.
Use the shards to cut through the skirt that the *other* human
described as
too short.
Who said your legs were *too fat,*
too skinny.
Who said you were *too loud,*
too quiet, too extra. Too proud,
 to make their words meaningful? Worthwhile?
Was the skirt too "feminine" or too "tempting?"
Too tempting to be feminine or what?

Was it the skirt that made him touch you *there?*
you know *there,*
the veiled part many want to see
but the sight insults larger audiences.
You know *there,*
the place the masses use to define you, *woman.*
You know there,
the open wound that causes so much pain.
Keep it open *it*
festers infectious names, *whore.*

keep it open *it*
doesn't belong to you,
it has a purpose, *mother.*
keep it open, he needs pleasure.
but also,
Close your legs.
Sit like a lady.
You're wearing a skirt.

I wonder,
who put a gap in the pay?
Can we close it?
There is a draught and
whoever opened it is too cold to feel it.
I am only trying to keep you warm and look pretty.

I thought you wanted an angel in the home.
The ideal *did say* clean.
Which culture should I start with?
Patriarchy or rape?

WOMEN'S ARCADE: PERSPECTIVE

Let me show you a thing called perspective.
Choose yourself a category from Women's Arcade
on the page to your right.
Paint the word on the front of your mind.
Wear it.
Look in the mirror for approximately,
every, second of the day.
If you do not have a mirror,
use the eyes of strangers to view your reflection.
Ensure to over-think the strangers expression.
Once you have selected a category remember,
this is now your identity.
Let it sink in.

If this brings you pleasure, then congratulations,
you understand the basic meaning of feminism,
and successfully exercised your freedom of choice.

If not and you feel victimised,
at any point during this activity
remember *you chose* the category.
You must now abide by the rules above.

PLEASE NOTE: To Play Women's Arcade you must experience the overwhelming desire to break the rules above.

To see extended rules please see page 116.

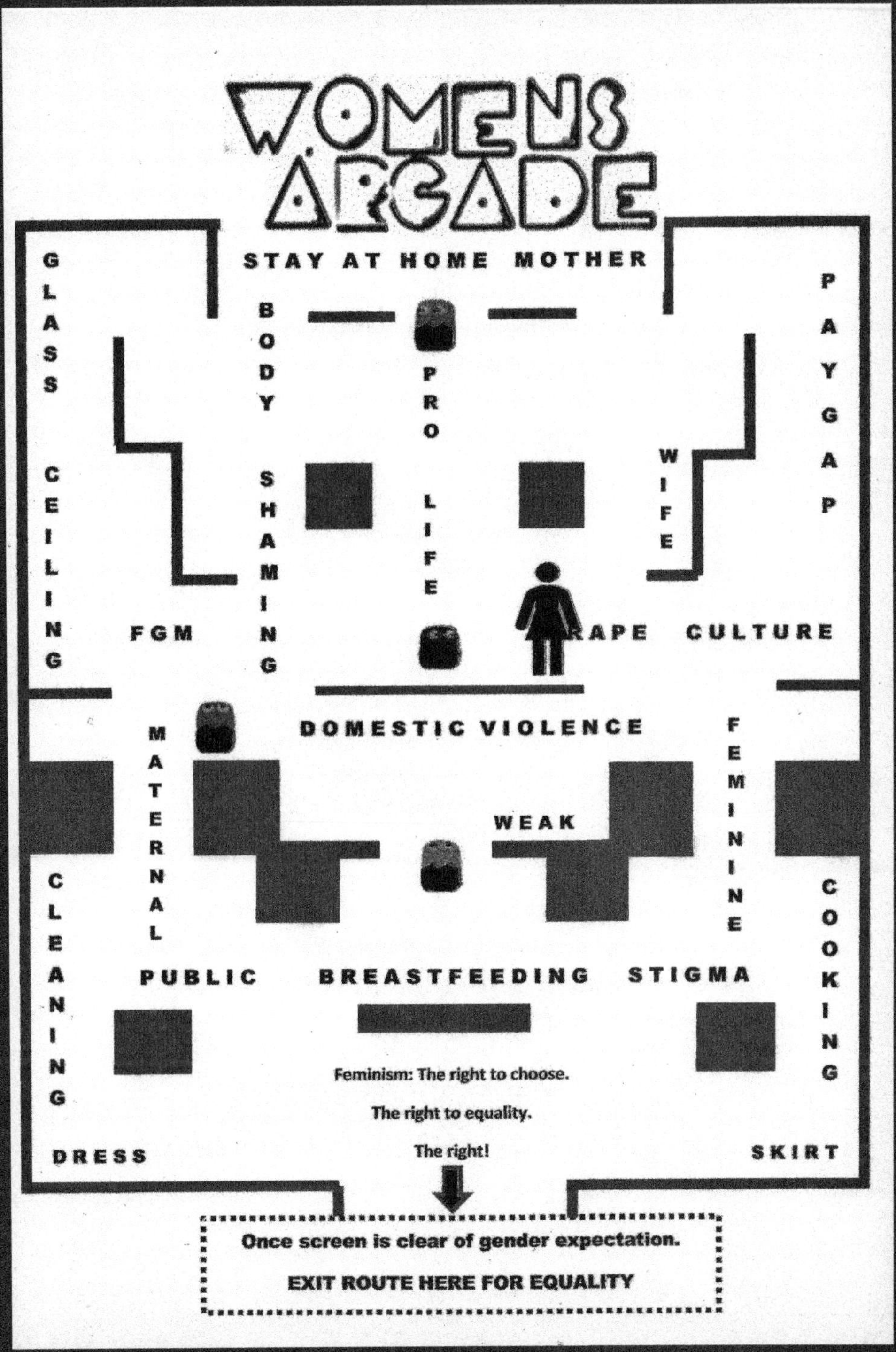
WOMENS ARCADE
STAY AT HOME MOTHER
GLASS CEILING
BODY SHAMING
PRO LIFE
WIFE
PAY GAP
FGM
RAPE CULTURE
DOMESTIC VIOLENCE
MATERNAL
FEMININE
WEAK
CLEANING
COOKING
PUBLIC BREASTFEEDING STIGMA
Feminism: The right to choose.
The right to equality.
The right!
DRESS
SKIRT
Once screen is clear of gender expectation.
EXIT ROUTE HERE FOR EQUALITY

WOMEN'S ARCADE: GAME ON

Game Rules:

Strip egotism, sexism and stereotyping from your flesh. This, by extension, will help to unhinge the ignorance which lays beneath. If ignorance is difficult to remove, knowledge may help to loosen the generational conditioning that fixed it there.

Once removed, you will experience what is known as an epiphanic state. This will reveal that the stereotype was not chosen. Your biology created the sex; patriarchy created the stereotype and, forcefully bound this to your identity.

During this revelation, you may experience symptoms of hopelessness and anger and wish to retaliate. If so, please fucking do so.

To win back your identity you must bite at the letters in the game, one by one. Eat them away and remove them from the screen to eradicate conformity.

You must escape the ghosts of patriarchy that veil the screen with *blissful ignorance* which is propelled by a long-standing history of gender discrimination.

Remember, the aim of the game is to eat away the stereotype, win back your freedom of choice and, most of all, survive.

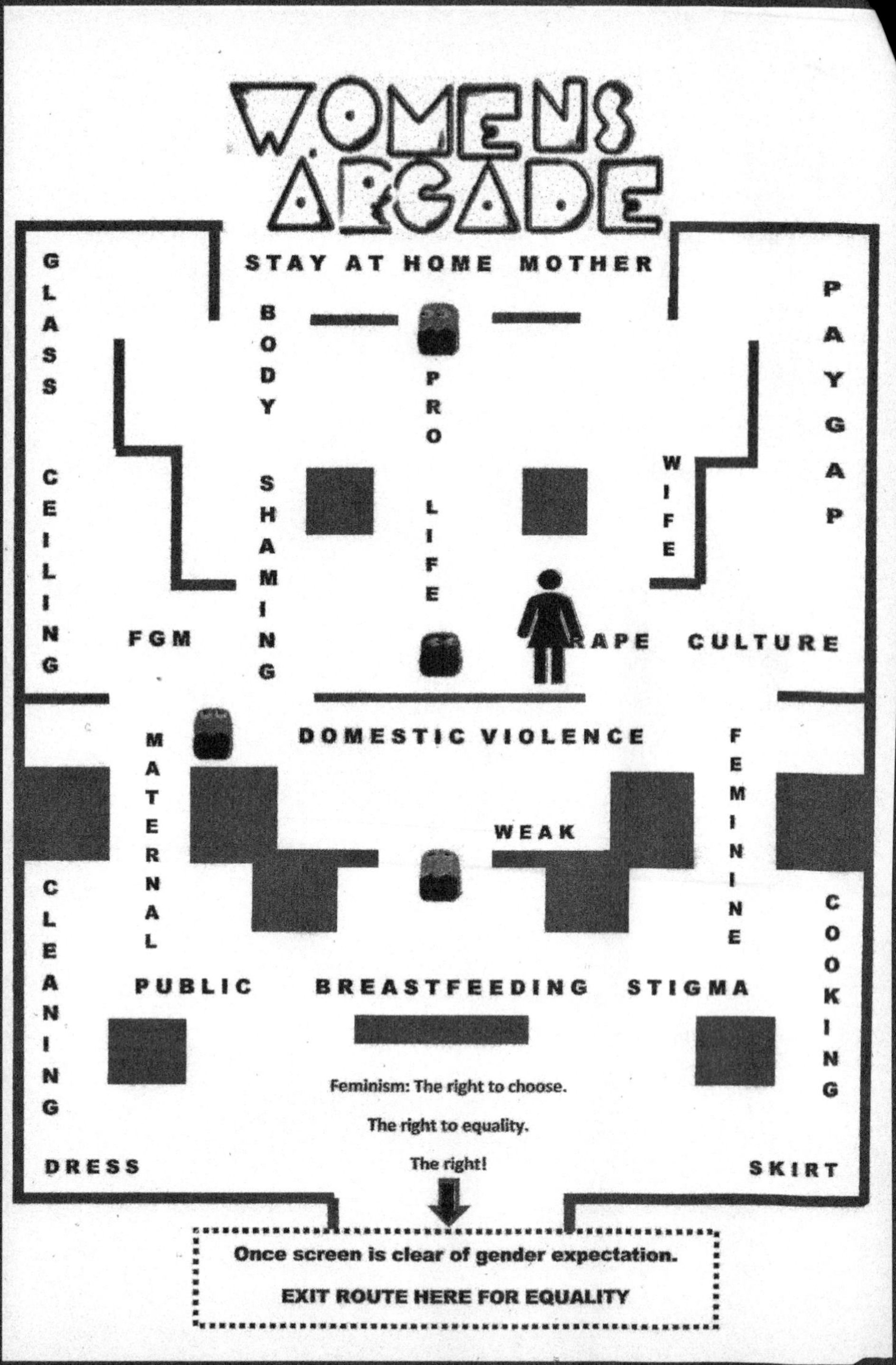

To Past Me

I have to let you go
We are now, and have been for a long time, two completely different people. I felt I needed to carry you with me. Wrap you in my arms and soak you in my flesh. Let your emotions become my own. We made a promise once. To protect each other. To fight together. I kept my promise and more.

I can't carry you any more. You are too heavy, become poison in my veins, skewed my perception of reality, layered skin so thick I can no longer feel, veiled my eyes so my days begin in darkness.

You don't belong inside me. You belong in the past. I can't advise you. But I can tell you, you have learned so much. You have grown. Trust me.
You are going to be OK.

Index

Page 7

 Lines taken from Anna Laetitia Barbauld's poem, The Rights of Woman (1792)

Bright, M., Ledger, S. and Egerton, G., 2006. *Keynotes And Discords*. London: Continuum, p.9.

Greenblatt, S., Lynch, D., Stillinger, J. and Burke, E., 2012. *The Norton Anthology Of English Literature*. New York: W.W. Norton, p.192.

James, H. and Luckhurst, R., 2009. *The Portrait Of A Lady*. Oxford: Oxford University Press, p.63.

Leitch, V. and Wollstonecraft, M., 1792. *The Norton Anthology Of Theory And Criticism*. New York, N.Y.: Norton, p.501.

Plath, Sylvia, 1963. The Bell Jar, p 46

Roberts, M., 2019. *Is There A Right Age To Lose Your Virginity?*. [online] BBC News. Available at: <https://www.bbc.co.uk/news/health-46794269> [Accessed 12 March 2020].

Woolf, V., 1929. *A Room Of One's Own*. London: Granada Publishing Limited, p.42.

Printed in Great Britain
by Amazon

59586791R00078